McPhers

McPherson

APPLES

FARM TO MARKET

Jason Cooper

Rourke Publications, Inc.
Vero Beach, Florida 32964

Edited by Pamela J.P. Schroeder

PHOTO CREDITS
All photos © Lynn M. Stone

Library of Congress Cataloging-in-Publication Data
Cooper, Jason, 1942-
    Apples / by Jason Cooper.
       p. cm. — (Farm to market)
    Summary: Describes how North American apples are grown,
processed, and shipped to consumers.
    ISBN 0-86625-622-9
    1. Apples—Juvenile literature. 2. Apple products—Juvenile
literature. 3. Apples—North America—Juvenile literature.
4. Apple products—North America—Juvenile literature.
[1. Apples.] I. Title. II. Series: Cooper, Jason, 1942-
Farm to market.
S6363.C77 1997
641.3741'1—dc21   97-13037
                                     CIP
                                     AC

Printed in the USA

TABLE OF CONTENTS

APPLES

Apples are not sold on branches, but that is where they begin their journey to market. They hang on short stems until they ripen. Then they drop off the branches or they are picked.

Apple farmers plant row upon row of apple trees in **orchards** (OR churdz). The trees may be more than 40 feet (12 meters) tall.

Apples are firm fruit covered by a smooth "skin," or peel. The apple's center, where the seeds are, is its core.

Most apples are ripe by fall. They will be picked from the branches, or drop to the ground.

KINDS OF APPLES

All apples belong to the rose family. Apple blossoms look very much like tiny, white or pink roses.

All apples, though, are not alike. Some are red. Others are yellow or green. Some apples have white fruit while others are cream-colored. Some apples are **tart** (TART). Others are quite sweet.

Thousands of kinds of apples grow around the world. In North America, most apples are red delicious, yellow delicious, Granny Smith, or MacIntosh.

These apples aren't red, but they are ripe. Some kinds of apples are green or yellow. These are yellow delicious.

WHERE APPLES GROW

Apple trees need fairly cold winters and warm summers. They do not grow well in very cold or very warm climates.

The United States is one of the world's biggest apple-growing countries. Among the states, Washington grows far more apples than the others. Michigan is the number two apple-growing state, followed by New York, California, and Pennsylvania.

In Canada, British Columbia grows the most apples.

Apple trees grow in areas with fairly cold winters. They need a time to "sleep," or be dormant.

PLANTING APPLE TREES

Almost all apple trees are grown from buds, rather than seeds. A bud is a type of growth on a twig. Farmers take buds and join them to the **rootstock** (ROOT stahk) of another tree. The rootstock is the stem and roots of a young tree. Farmers choose rootstock that grows well in the area where it is being planted.

The "new" tree grows the same kind of apples as the bud tree. Meanwhile, the rootstock gives the new tree a head start.

These young apple trees had a quick start by growing from buds and rootstocks joined together.

Day's work done, apple buckets rest on their treasures.

Apple farmers keep beehives nearby. As bees move, they spread pollen.
Pollen helps fruit begin to grow.

GROWING APPLES

Each spring apple trees produce thousands of blossoms. Bees visit the blossoms and help **pollinate** (POL in ate) them. After being pollinated, the blossoms begin to grow into apples.

Apples and trees have many enemies—insects, mites, and **fungus** (FUN gus), to name a few. Farmers sometimes spray the orchard with chemicals to kill the pests.

Meanwhile, the apples grow and ripen. Most varieties, or kinds, of apples ripen in 20 to 24 weeks.

Bees help pollinate apple blossoms in spring. Blossoms soon disappear and tiny, growing apples take their place.

HARVESTING APPLES

Farmers begin to harvest apples in late August. Most apples are harvested during the fall. Each variety ripens at a different time.

Farmers pick apples by hand. Pickers climb ladders to reach high branches. They put apples into crates and load them into trucks, which take the apples away.

Many orchards sell apples directly to buyers, like supermarkets. Farmers put some apples into cold storage, where they stay fresh for up to a year.

An apple orchard owner picks a bag of ripe red delicious apples in late October.

PROCESSING APPLES

About four apples of every 10 are shipped by truck from orchards to apple-processing plants, or factories.

There apples are **processed** (PRAH sest), or changed, into different forms. Apples may be cut up or crushed. They may be canned, dried, or frozen.

Processing plants change apples into many products. Most of them we know well.

A young lady sorts apples for bagging at an orchard.

APPLE PRODUCTS

Fresh apples may be ground into tangy cider. Cider is cloudy because it has tiny pieces of apple in it. Apple juice is clear. It is strained and heat-treated at an apple-processing plant.

Apples are also used in apple pies, apple butter, jellies, cereal, snacks, applesauce, wine, and pastries.

Sweet apples are usually sold for "eating" apples. Many tart apple varieties are used in processed apple foods. Mixtures of different apples make great cider and pies.

Apple processing plants—and good cooks—make many tasty apple products.

ACKS

HY SWEETENED THREE-GRAIN CEREAL
WITH APPLE & CINNAMON

Quality
Guaranteed
Jewel
100% PURE
APPLE JUICE
FROM CONCENTRATE

NET 64 FL OZ (2 QT) 1.89 L

SELMAN'S

MUSSELMAN'S

NATURAL

APPLE SAUCE

NET WT 23 OZ (1 LB 7 OZ) 652 g

APPLES AS FOOD

"An apple a day keeps the doctor away" is an old saying. It has some truth to it.

Apples are a healthy food. They are made up of water, mostly, but they also have plenty of **nutrients** (NU tree ents). Nutrients in food are what's good for us. Apples have nutrients like vitamins A, C, B-1, and B-2.

Apples give a good energy boost, and they have fiber. Fiber helps your body process the foods you already ate.

Glossary

fungus (FUN gus) — a group of living plantlike things, some of which are harmful to plants or animals

nutrient (NU tree ent) — any of several "good" substances that the body needs for health, growth, and energy; vitamins and minerals

orchard (OR churd) — a place where many apple trees, or other fruit trees, are raised

pollinate (POL in ate) — to transfer pollen grains from one plant to another

processed (PRAH sest) — changed in form or moved from one place to another; prepared for market

rootstock (ROOT stahk) — the root system and stem of a tree that is joined with a bud from another tree

tart (TART) — a fresh, sharp taste

INDEX